A Beautiful
Hallucination

Emma Laing

Outskirts Press, Inc.
Denver, Colorado

Dedication

To my parents who deserve far more than this book

"Look beyond the obvious."
~Richard Erikson

Table of Contents

Some Things

I did not teach you
So I don't know how…

You learned to read
My chipped red nail polish
Like the Morse code
No one had yet
Been able to decipher.

You learned to listen
To the undeniable "ping"
Each time I connected my ring
To a glass bottle half full
(And never empty.)

You learned to seduce
Me with your words-
Dangling participles mercilessly
In front of my eyes
Then snatching them away
With nouns and verbs
To feed the soul.

You learned to lie
To me with the curves
Of your body
And the corners
Of your smile.
You learned to love
Me like it was
Going out of style.
You learned to breathe
In sync with my dreams
Like darkness
With the setting sun.

You learned to sleep
Next to me

Oh so perfectly
That the man on the moon
Blew us kisses
As slumber stole our spirits
For the stars in the skies.

You learned to sing
Tone deaf lullabies that
Tore into me like
God humming symphonies.

You learned to explore
My body with your lips
Like sonar on the ocean floor
Until with eyes closed
And lips parted
You could plot
Every
Last
Point.

But I learned something too.

I learned to make none of that
Mean anything to me
Because when sadness and pleasure
Are so close together
It's hard to tell the difference.

So as I am sitting,
Bottled inspiration sipping,
And short stanza spitting
I can't help thinking
It would be nice to forget you,
Pretend I never met you,

But there are some things
I'll never learn.

Moe.

Vibes penetrate even the paralyzed
As the stillest we stay
Is the first time we rise
We could drink the Milky Way
With the thirst in our eyes

Souls are quenched when
Carefully crafted guitar licks
Our necks
And no matter where it begins
It's always too quick
To end.

I Hope You Understand

No matter how many times I say it
It still means nothing

I love you, I love you, I love you

A phrase
Three words
Eight letters
It's nothing but
Eight letters
Three words
A phrase

I love you, I love you, I love you

I is selfish
Love is an enigma
And you are perfect

I love you, I love you, I love you

My soul would sing emotions to you
If I knew how to make it,
But my soul is voiceless
And words are all we have
So I hope you understand when I say:

I love you, I love you, I love you

But in case you don't…
Just surround me with your arms
Like the body does the soul,
And if you squeeze really tight
And listen really close
You'll hear my heart hum a lullaby
And then you'll know

I love you, I love you, I love you.

Fragments

Glorious
Is the only word for someone

Who takes apart his soul
And hands out a piece
To everyone he meets

Hoping that he will be
Reassembled
Upon conclusion

And

Knowing that it will have been
Worth it
No matter what.

Middle School Romance

Day by day she convinces herself
Everything will be okay in the end,
But she doesn't want to wait that long.

No matter how hard she closes her eyes
He can still see her,
No matter how hard she tries not to sing along
She'll forever know the lyrics
To their song.
She fails to erase
His mannequin smile
Pointing invisible guns
At empty heads
Becomes a sick pastime
As she stares with empty eyes at
Empty eyes.
Writing his name in her notebook
Turns into carving his face
On her arm with a knife,
But pain is never enough
And so she gives up.
Sleep is her painkiller,
But her body won't let her
Become addicted, not again,
Her body knows her better than her mind.
And so she cries.
She cries for herself and a little for him
And she doesn't care who sees.
A hand closes around her shoulder
And it's familiar at first
Then distant.
Each curve of her body the fingers touch
Burns with sadness and
Bruises with time.
She doesn't need to turn
Since his face is already
Engraved in her mind and so
She closes her eyes.

All I Ask

I am out of my heart
And my mind is broken

I am a collected mess
Of words unspoken,
A rancid pile of coffee grinds,
Expired leftovers of all kinds,
Used tissues and unwanted treasures
Abandoned haphazardly
In the rubbish bin that is me.

I'm overfull with the ethereal
And I'm begging to be emptied.

Please gut and discard my poetry
So that I am free
To find my heart
And fix my mind
Before I am out of time.

Can I Write Poetry About You?

His warm breath wraps gently
Around her vulnerable neck
And she wants to say "I love you"
Instead she closes her eyes
And pictures his.

He kisses her cheek
And calls her beautiful
And she wants to say "you're perfect"
Instead she squeezes his hand
And smiles.

He glides down her back
As she listens to his spirit
And she wants to say "never let go"
Instead she hides her head
On top of his heart.

He whispers "can I write poetry about you?"
And she wants to scream "yes!"
Her soul wants to break free
Of her body and hold him
But instead she manages
"It's only fair, I write about you".

Rev

Could you taste the thirst in me
To bring out the worst in you?

Even before you kissed me
I already missed you.

My Bob Dylan Lullabies

His fingers danced across the neck of his guitar
Like they were John Travolta in Pulp Fiction
And the guitar was just another stage for him to act
upon.
I never actually watched him play.
His silhouette reflected on my bedroom door
As he sat just outside
Like a mirror he refused to look in.
But the image his shadow projected
Still made him the biggest man I had ever seen.
The lyrics echoed off walls in my head
Teaching me about changing times,
Blowing wind, and heaven's door.
To me he never stopped playing.
I was always asleep before he was finished
His voice became the soundtrack of my dreams.

Imagine Perfection

Since the moment he could hold things
His hands searched for something they loved
Because he wanted to find the one thing
His hands would never let go.

Since the moment she could wear skirts
Her hips searched for something they loved
Because she wanted to find the one thing
Her hips would wear best.

When his hands met her hips
He never let go
And she never wore anything better.

Fleeing Gods

In a world
Where humankind is so blind
We don't even realize
The Gods have fled,
The incomprehensible beauty
Of the human spirit
Seems also to have hidden
Inside realities divisions
Masked by nature's dilutions
And revealed by human confusion.

We need to stop
Imposing sanity on chaos
And futilely ordering
This primordial mess
Lennon said it best:
Let it be.

A Moment at the Gathering of the Vibes

I'm surrounded by ultimate Frisbee, dreadlocks,
And dirty feet with Birkenstocks
So I lie on back as the sky sings to me
Because God decided to let himself free
And forgot for a moment who he had to be.

God and I took a break together that sunny summer afternoon
We smoked a few cloves
And he explained to me the path that he chose.
He said, "With good there must be evil
And with happiness one must be sad,
So in order to fill the earth that I had
I began with everything bad."

He paused to take another drag
And surveyed the magical scene;
Women danced with arms open wide
And men with eyes closed tight.

God held back tears with all of his might,
"I don't want rain to fall
On such a beautiful day,
But it's tears of joy
So the sun will stay."

The colors of God's tie-dyed shirt slowly began to run
As his tears baptized the dancers below,
Grateful to be in the sun.

God put out the clove and turned to me,
"It's not as easy as it seems to create evil beings,

But it's the price I chose to pay
So these people could have today.
First I thought of the lowest of lows
Then put those things on earth,
Next I thought of the highest of highs
And created dancing in the sunshine."
God winked at me and added,
"While drinking aged red wine."

He apologized for all he'd done to cause fear, death,
and pain
But said He hoped it was worth it for all that we
could gain.

"It's time for me to get back to work
And see what I can do
To make this world closer to perfect
For every one of you."

God kissed my cheek and waved goodbye
As I turned back over and opened by eyes
I saw crowds in front and a stage even farther.
Now everyday I pray God work just a bit harder
To show evil people how happy they can be
If they take just one moment to dance with me.

Soul Garden

I'm not sure why I let you into
The garden of my soul,
But something told me
That you would hold me
While you mold me
Into a garden
Worthy of Eden.

Your whispers weeded
What I thought I needed
And you succeeded
As my heart pleaded
For pure perfection.

Then you planted seeds
Of unborn roses
That would soon
Sprout wings,
Learn to sing,
And eventually:
To sting.

Your kisses like sunlight
Nurtured my soul,
Your caresses so sweet
Were miracle grow,
Your tongue fed me
And I kneaded you like dough.
I needed you like oxygen
Not caring where you'd been
As long as you kept me alive.

Soon the roses bloomed fully
With perfect petals
They began to settle.
As roots crept deeper
I wanted to explore
All that was yours,
But then I remembered

Roses have thorns.
Too bad our timeline
Was so short
To you I resign
As a last resort.

My soul was desperate and you revived it,
My body on yours was an exact fit,
You were the one I wanted to get,
And even though roses have thorns I must admit
I liked their prick just a bit.

Poetry

Between the lines of an old, torn notebook

Or glaring typed and double-spaced on a new PC

Poetry is more than an A B A B rhyme scheme

More than Walt Whitman or Robert Frost
And their personal thoughts.

Poetry is beyond description

It is not the stark impenetrable dark of the pupil in
her eye

Nor the blood red stain on solid cement from the
fall of a small child.

Kelcie's House

It's the place to go when there's nowhere to go
And the place to go when you could go anywhere
It's the place to go when you need some advice
And the place to go to forget your life
If those walls could talk, we'd keep them quiet
Because the bed's never made, but we still lie in it
We discuss philosophy and put on the Dead
We go on journeys that are all in our heads
It's just another night listening to Phish
We go back to school and good times are missed
It's where laughter and love heal better than band-aids
And our friendships may shake, but they'll never fade
We reminisce about plights overcome in the past
We know with each story it isn't the last
Where more cigarettes are smoked than breaths of fresh air
And where stories about romance are always shared
It's the place to go after the best day of the year
And the place to go after a day filled with fear
It's the place that none of us will ever forget
And it's the place where you and I first met
So next time there is nowhere to be
Come chill here with us and let your soul free.

Almost Anything

I'll give you my word
And you can keep the change
As long as you drop the pennies
For unsuspecting luckies to find
Because I'll give almost anything
For a smile.

Heartbreaker

He requires a job that needs no application
Just the ability to sell drugs to a nation
Of children growing up too fast.

And all he really wants is someone
To make love to his soul.

It is fitting that it is done in lines
Since lines on a plane are continuous
And once you snort just one
It doesn't end there.

Eventually he offers his spirit for collateral
And finally enough is enough
So I ask him to stop.

He simply grinds his tender, tired teeth
And responds,
SNIFF, SNIFF

It's Been Too Long

Do you remember gnawing on knowledge at a
narrator's house?
Or discussing poetry with our minds and mouths
closed?
I remember putting up blinds on your eyes
Because they say eyes are the windows to the soul
And I did not want you getting chilly.
What about when we changed the world,
But it kept on turning slowly?
Remember when the world changed us,
But we kept on being lonely?
I remember never wanting to be so vulnerable that
I'd melt in someone's arms
That is, until you showed me what it felt like to melt
in yours.
Did you forget the colors of the sky when we
changed our minds?
Or did you forget the day he died and the closure
we could not find?
I forgot how much we laughed until I dreamt of
your smile;
Did you know it changes lives?
It's certainly altered mine.
Do you remember when we were best friends?
Did you know that it would ever end?
I remember the day that they sent you away
And I could not give you a hug goodbye.

I know it's absurd to ask questions of someone who
needs answers,
But do you remember the last time I saw you?
We were in the seventh grade and the hopeful sun
was shining,
Your parents were angry and your sister was
whining.
They threw you in the car and said you weren't
coming back.
I'm sure someday I'll see you again,
I just hope that when I do you remember.

[21]

I'm Trying

I know I will never
Be able to write
A poem
That will change
People's lives,
But I'm still trying
All the time
To write just
One poem
That will change mine.

The Music Says It All

He eased us out of insignificant silence the moment
he held his guitar.
I tried to avert my eyes, but quickly became
mesmerized by the way his hands danced
Each note of complicated choreography flowed
flawlessly into the next
He was God creating an endless universe suspended
within a song.
He played as effortlessly as I listened and I don't
know whether it was
The beauty of his calloused hands or the ease of his
tranquil lips
That made me float, but I think it was his eyes.
The music captivated my body and I was
completely still where I sat
So my soul had to do all the dancing, but it was
okay with that.
Eventually he played softly and spoke even softer,
"I wrote that song for you"
His embarrassed eyes apologized as though it were
imperfect
Then he asked me to forgive the lack of lyrics.
But the music says it all, I thought.
"The music's not enough," he whispered, "but I
could never put you into words."

Tuesday Night at Home

I never wanted to be so exposed
That I'd feel at home
In anyone's arms other than my own
Until I spent a night in yours.

In your arms
I felt an irresistible comfort
Like dry socks on wet feet
Warm against your sweatshirt
Liquor breathes so sweet,
I felt unspeakably safe
Your chest as my shield
Your hands as my brace
Only dreams concealed
Behind a somber face.

And in your arms
It's nice to know
That I will never be
Home alone.

Not Forgotten

A graceful tattoo on inky hips
Bleeds through unmoving lips
As chapped tongue shamefully licks
Cocaine credit cards to get a fix…

Roundabout

I wish that I could show you
How I draw you like a bath
Then soak in euphoria
While I cleanse myself
With your aura.

I want to be a syllable
That makes souls skip
I want to be a word
As beautiful as an eclipse
I want to be a phrase
Dangling from your lips.

I am a stone gargoyle
Until your kiss makes it night,
Breathes life into me,
And freezes time
At twilight.

So here's my roundabout way
To hold you close and say:
I love you.

Waiting for Rain

Rain's song drowns my worries
And it's dance keeps them down.
My suffocating problems collide and bruise
Then spiral in every direction.
When the rain stops
My mind is a pool of cadavers,
But even though dead bodies float
And water evaporates
The mass grave that is my brain
Cannot wait for it to rain.

Life Lessons

It's easier to build a pyramid from lost loves
Than it is to lose another,
It's easier to change the world
Than it is to hate your brother.

It's harder to have false friendships
Than it is to be alone,
It's harder to let happiness slip away
Than it is to lose all that you own.

It's better to tell them "I love you"
Than it is to assume they know,
It's better to try everything once
Than it is to say no.

It's worse to ignore the truth
Than it is to tell a lie,
It's worse to keep it all inside
Than it is to let someone see you cry.

Who said you learn nothing in high school?

An Autumn Night

It was so cold
The air was thick with emptiness
But inhaling nothing is effortless
I consumed every word
That left your contorted mouth
Now I forget them all, but I remember
You were so warm.

Sunday Mornings

We wake up
To bodies that have been
Shaken
And served on the rocks
While our souls have been
Stirred
And served up, with a twist.

We dig for memories
Of the night before
And unearth fossils
In the form of
Digital pictures
And we laugh
And laugh
And laugh.

We start drinking
At point A
A is for apathetic
And stop drinking
At point B
B is for blackout.

Liquidating life
Is so much easier
Than living it.
But come Sunday mornings
We cannot help but long
To find the long nights lost.

The problem:
We don't know where to look.

But come Saturday nights
The bottles whisper our names
With such an enticing appeal
We cannot help but long
To hold them again
So we drink
And drink
And drink.

Caught Red Lipped

She leaves a trail of lipstick everywhere she goes,
Which makes his detective work very easy.

In the morning a red stain appears on her coffee cup
As she guzzles a new beginning.
In the afternoon a red tattoo pierces her
All too necessary cigarette.
And in the evening red rings make their way
Across her many martini glasses.
But her lipstick never leaves its mark
On one desirable place.

His lips
They would look much better
Tinted red.

Numbers

Accompanied by stars
In the skies, in your eyes
I was an island
Surrounded by your arms
On an island
Surrounded by the ocean
Ever-lapping in a motion
As if challenging us
To a duel.

Duel meaning two
One was me
And one was you
A pair of dice rolled snake eyes
On an island called Paradise.

Together we were two
And to a small mind two
Is a small number,
But with hearts as big as ours
Two is twice the size of one,
Which is more than double
One unforgettable night.

Mouths and Dreams

Dry mouths and wet dreams
Invade my high school memories

While empty mouths and infinite dreams
Are the foundation of my college's

I hope eventually for memories
Of smiling mouths and fulfilled dreams.

Too Good to Be False

You're my over-inspirational muse.
I know some authors write about heartache and booze,
But you're the only outlet I can use.
I've already crafted novels from the colors in your eyes
And given birth to poetry conceived in the womb of your smile.
I've written about your hair, your hands, and your heart
I touch pen to paper and your lips are where I start.
I guess I have too much to say about you
Because you're the perfect over-inspirational muse.
I know some authors write about heartache and booze,
But you're the only outlet I'd ever choose.
There's not enough music on earth for me to compose your song,
But once all pens are out of ink
And all the lyrics have been sung,
I'll close my eyes and think of you
My over-inspirational muse.

Subliminal Hate

Breeding grounds of hate
Become bleeding grounds
Coated with crimson dirt.

Broken weapons and
Broken hearts
Glued together with fear
And anticipation of death
Or worse, or better.

Death may not be so bad
If the only other choice
Is living.

Stupid Love Poem

When I am alone,
I miss the mirage
His fingertips create
On the surface of my still body.
When I am awake,
I long to sleep
So I can dream of his
Soul-soaked hands.
When I am afraid,
And whispers are eternal
I inhale his eyes
As they reflect mine.
When I am with him,
I listen to his silhouette dance
And watch the silent suffocation
Of his smile.
I consume his distilled shadows
And feel the beat of his
Bruised heart
While I float through my mind.
When I am alone I miss,
When I am awake I long,
When I am afraid I inhale,
When I am with him
I listen and watch,
I consume and feel,
When I am with him
I float.

Illusion

Conceived deep in his throat,
Born through the womb
On the tip of his tongue
Simply by inhaling
He expects to consume
His already exhaled past.
His contorted ideas
Soar from the tomb
Of shadows and lies,
But despite what happened
He will forever loom
Over the same mistake.
He is not empty
Just alone in his room
Wanting less than he has.
Some flowers strive
Not to bloom.

Clearly

This is clearly your destiny
Don't fight it, just let it be.
Just close your eyes and realize
That you were born to die.

Black Coffee

She stares into her 10:37 cup of hotel coffee
And feels she is the little red straw:
Free of charge, available to be chewed on.

Feeling useless she stares deeper,
Making eye contact with herself
She blows slowly into the black coffee
And smiles at her newly distorted face.

As the steam rushes back at her
She shuts her eyes and they refuse to reopen
As she falls hard into a dizzying state.

Her complementary hotel coffee leaves her hand
And lands painfully on the pre-stained rug.

A few drops splash on her exposed legs
And she allows them to singe her skin.

Her eyes eventually agree to open
As she directs them towards the clock
It reads 10:39, which is perfect timing.

What Have I Gotten Myself Into?

I've known him for
Two hours
And he's already
Too much
For me ever
To forget.
I close my eyes
And am mesmerized
As his head floats
In mine.
I shut them tighter
And the vision gets lighter
But then I hear
His whisper.
I block my ears,
Which quells my fears
Until I feel his face
By mine.
I pull myself away
As my mind begins to stray
To the scent of his soft,
Sweet skin.
I pinch my nose
And inadvertently curl my toes
As the taste of his lips
Infiltrates mine.
A mouth that I am yet to kiss
But somehow I already miss
The mirage of his
Honey lips.

52

The smell of childhood escapes
Every time you open your eyes
In sync with your tears and the rain
You desperately shuffle the defenseless deck of
cards
Doing all you can to revive them
Praying with enough movement they will live
Watching one of them flutter to the ground
With the weight of all your fears
Your head of stone debates the next signal
To send to the tips of your still fingers
Your arm reaches out to enclose the world
In the palm of your sweat-soaked hand
But you miss and the cards crash to the
Worn out floor of the silent room
Lunging to hold on to any part of yourself
Your body becomes limp and useless
As it falls to the floor in sync with your tears
And the rain

For Your Next Long Trip

He says he wants to pack me as his pillow
When he goes away.
He would hold me all night long
And I would stay awake to protect him from
nightmares
(I would no longer need to dream
Of the one I wished was beside me).

Then I would watch him sleep
Because no matter how many forevers I have stared
at his face
I could never get bored of it.
There is always more to explore.

I would be happy all the time just being near him
Because I could spend eternities doing nothing
(As long as he was by my side).

I would be the best damn pillow in the world
Because if I'm gonna do it- I'll make it happen.
He deserves nothing but the best
And even the best isn't enough sometimes
For someone who can change my world with his
eyes.
He would lean on me and tell me everything
But pillows can't talk back.
So as much as I'd love to be a pillow for perfects
I need to be more than that.

Imperfect Fit

It would be easier
If you could walk in my shoes,
But they wouldn't quite fit you.
With your swollen feet
And my tired hands
Together we would make
A perfect aged couple…
It's too bad we're too young
To be old enough
To know better,
But I do know worse
And I wish you could fit
In my shoes.

Memo

She traces her tragic life on sheets of paper
Securing substance with every stroke of her pen.
With no boundaries, none are ever broken.
She obediently stays in vacant lines
Without complaint or protest
Color after color, delicately fading
And slipping away unnoticed
Some blending with others
Integrating into artistic shades
Only to be quickly erased from existence.
The sky is blue, the grass: green
Very little remains in the middle.
Time passes and her paper wrinkles
Each crease descending deeper
Etched within her redundant mind.
It is no longer of meaning at all
A paper crushed and dirty,
A pen run dry of ink,
A faint outline of once bright colors
Lifeless, useless, and void of memories
If only it had been worth preserving.

On Befriending a Teacher

I thought I had knocked on heaven's door when a teacher took my hand.
His eyes advised history while his lips declared legend
As he led me up an unsuspecting hill and through a beach littered with memories.
His tactful winks and unpredictable smiles told the future
As he led me through moments both past and present.
He conducted captivating classes on confidence and conscience
Then assigned happiness for homework and made it due once a day.
He taught me to live life fully because there's no excuse to lose a dream
And he taught me to love life fully because there's no price on borrowed time.
I thought I had knocked on heaven's door when a teacher took my hand;
I knew I had knocked on something better when a friend embraced my mind.

About the Author

Emma Laing is a college student who lives in Ipswich, Massachusetts. Her poetry has been published in a variety of works including *Pegasus*, *The Henniker Review*, and <u>Reflections</u>. <u>A Beautiful Hallucination</u> is her first collection of poetry.